Today's Singapore

Photography By Goh Tianwah

First published July 2001

Rank Books
Blk 1002 Toa Payoh Ind Pk #07-1423
Singapore 319074
Tel: 65-2508180 Fax: 65-2506191
Website: www.rankbooks.com
Email: admin@rankbooks.com

ISBN 981-04-3968-7

Photography and text by Goh Tianwah
Copyright © Rank Books

Cover-design and typeset by Rank Publishing

Colour separation by Colourscan Co Pte Ltd
Printed By Tien Wah Press Pte Ltd

CONTENTS

A Short History of Singapore

In 1819, Sir Stamford Raffles of the British's East India Company set up a trading post in Singapore under an agreement signed between the Sultan of Johore and the Malay ruler of the island. In 1824, the British gained full control of Singapore and the island was ceded in perpetuity to East India Co by the Johore Sultan. It came under the rule of British colonial office until the year 1959 when Singapore held its first general election. The People's Action Party, led by Lee Kuan Yew, won 43 seats out of 51 seats. The first government of the state of Singapore was formed and Lee Kuan Yew became Singapore's first Prime Minister. In 1963, Singapore decided to join the Federation of Malaya which had gained full independence from the British since 1957. The merger led to the formation of Malaysia comprising the Federation of Malaysia (11 Malaysian states), Singapore, Sarawak, and North Borneo (now known as Sabah). The merger resulted in many problems and disputes. On 9th August 1965, Singapore separated from Malaysia to become an independent Republic.

3. Statue of Sir Stamford Raffles, the founder of Singapore. This figure stands on North Boat Quay, behind the old Parliament House where Raffles is believed to have landed in 1819.

Singapore Today

From a small island with no natural resources and racked with unemployment in the 1960s to a thriving modern city-state with one of the highest incomes in Asia in less than 30 years, was no mean feat. Many world leaders had described Singapore's economic success as a miracle of the century. It deserved to be the role model for the world. Since the 1980s until today, Singapore has scored a number of tops in the world, including the world's busiest port, the world's highest savings rate among other achievements.

Top In The World

1. The world's highest rate of national saving with the world's fourth highest per capital income.
2. Singapore is among the top five countries in the world with the largest foreign exchange reserve.
3. Singapore has the best port in Asia and it is the world's busiest containers port.
4. Singapore's Changi Airport is voted by the world's leading travellers magazines as the best airport in the world.
5. Singapore is the world's 16th largest trading nation.
6. Singapore Airlines is voted as the best airline in the world by the Travel Trade Gazette.
7. Singapore was rated the third best Asian city for business by Fortune magazine.
8. Singapore was rated the third best Asian city to live in by Asiaweek magazine.
9. In the latest world competitive yearbook, Singapore retains its overall standing as the second most competitive economy after United States of America.
10. Five of Singapore's hotels have made it to the world's top 80 hotels with Raffles Hotel in second spot according to the latest annual ranking by the Institute of Investor.

5. A panoramic view of Singapore waterfront as seen from Marina Bay.

6. The new Parliament building at the junction of High Street and North Bridge Road was completed in 1999 with a gross floor area of 19,765 sq.m, five times larger than the old parliament house located less than a minute's walk away.

8. The Supreme Court was designed in the late 1930s by Frank Dorrington. It is the last classical building to be built in Singapore. Standing tall at the center of the building's exterior are six Corinthian columns supporting the pediment sculpture (as an allegory of justice) created by Cavalieri Rodolfo Nolli, an Italian artist who was also a sculptor and contractor.

9. A bird's eye view of the Singapore River.

7. The Istana House, situated at the end of Orchard Road is the official residence of the Republic's President. It is also used as the Prime Minister's office. The Istana is opened to the public on certain public holidays such as New Year's Day, Chinese New Year and Deepavali.

10. Old buildings are not forgotten in a city where towering skyscrapers predominates. In many parts of the city, old buildings stand in harmony with the new, breaking the monotony of the typical urban landscape. In the background are rows of old shop houses along North Bridge Road with the towering skyscrapers of Suntec City.

11. Old shop houses at North Boat Quay which used to be shops and offices of merchants, traders and those in the shipping business.

12. Another view of the Singapore River as seen from the swimming pool on the rooftop of Fullerton Hotel. This luxury hotel was officially opened on 31 December 2000 by the Prime Minister of Singapore, Mr Goh Chok Tong.

13A. The Westin Stamford Hotel - The World's tallest hotel boasts of 70 storeys.
13B. Raffles Place, the major banking and financial district in Singapore.

14. Glitz, ritz and glamour: Five world-class hotels form the landmark of Marina Bay. From right to left: The Ritz-Carlton, The Oriental, The Pan Pacific, Conrad International Centennial and Marina Mandarin. Each of these hotels offers stunning view of the Singapore waterfront.

15. This picture shows four 45-storey office towers of Suntec City which were built with state-of-the-art technology and based on Chinese fengsui. All buildings in Suntec City were built to generate good fortune and harmony. Viewed from the top, the five office towers of Suntec City resemble the human left hand, with the 18-storey Suntec City Tower representing the thumb, and the four 45-storey office towers the fingers. The fountain plaza is like a gold ring placed in the center of the palm. The Singapore International Convention & Exhibition Centre represents the wrist.

16. Orchard Road is a shopper's paradise and one of Singapore's main attractions. Lots of greenery and trees adorn both sides of the street, offering shoppers natural shades from the tropical sun. The Orchard Road experience is not complete without some serious people-watching.

17. Ngee Ann City, one of the largest shopping mall in Orchard Road, houses many local and foreign fashion boutiques. Takashimaya, the Japanese departmental store which occupies most of the building's floor area, is a favourite spot for Japanese tourists.

Singapore From The Air

Viewing Singapore from the air is an exhilarating experience. You cannot help but sense the speed of progress and modernisation that has taken place in such a small island over such a short span of time.

18. An aerial view of Victoria Theatre with the Empress Place next to it. Empress Place, constructed between 1864-65. was named after Queen Victoria.

19. An aerial view of Singapore River beginning from Boat Quay to Clarke Quay. In the 1840s, the buildings on both banks of the river were dominated by trading offices and warehouses of merchants and traders.

20. Aerial view of the rows of old shop houses in Chinatown area.

21. A spectacular view of the Padang, Suntec City and Marina Square from the air. This picture shows the Singapore flag being carried by two military helicopters flying above Suntec City towards the Padang where the National Day celebration was held on 9th Aug 2000.

22. A bird's eye view of the old shop houses at Neil Road and the Tanjong Pagar area. Most of the shop houses in these areas were built from the 1890s to the 1920s. Today, these buildings are restored and conserved under the government's conservation plan.

23. Another aerial view of the Central Business District.

24. Toa Payoh Town was one of the earliest estate built by the Housing and Development Board in the 1960s.

25. An aerial view of the area from Balestier Road and southwards to the Central Business District area. The unique building with a golden stupa on its roof at the bottom of this picture is the Burmese Buddhist Temple situated at Tai Jin Road.

Singapore At Night

The island transforms itself from a garden city in the day to a glamorous city of glittering lights after sunset. Since Singapore is one of the world's safest cities at night, it offers many alluring possibilities from alfresco dining, pub-hopping, to a quiet romantic stroll in the city. After dark, the pubs and restaurants in areas such as Boat Quay, Clarke Quay, Tanjong Pagar and Mohamad Sultan Road burst into life, offering diners and party-goers a place to eat and unwind.

26A. A view of the Singapore waterfront from the Esplanade Bridge which is also an ideal spot for a romantic stroll.

26B. Suntec City's Fountain of Wealth is also known as the World's Largest Fountain as recorded in the 1998 edition of the Guinness Book of Records. The circular shape of the fountain with water gushing inwards symbolises a ring in the palm of the hand, guaranteeing the retention of wealth.

27. Dazzling street lights along the Esplanade Bridge.

28. The Central Business District area at night.

29. The majestic Fullerton Hotel as seen from Cavenagh Bridge.

30. After sunset, Clarke Quay embraces a festive atmosphere as it becomes a huge night bazaar filled with push-carts selling traditional food like spicy chilli crabs and satay (Malay Kebabs), along with the many restaurants and bars.

31. Neon lights from the many restaurants and pubs at Boat Quay, plus special lighting from the skyscrapers around the area, set the Singapore River ablaze with lights after dark.

32 and 33. A stunning view of the Singapore waterfront at night.

34. The Pan-Island Expressway is 42-kilometres long and it connects the eastern and western parts of Singapore.

35. A breadth-taking aerial view around Marina Bay. Nearby ships in the harbour can be seen on the right of this picture. Golden streaks of light on the left of the picture is East Coast Parkway, one of the major highways that connects the island.

Restoration Of A City

Old buildings are records of history and they provide the young and future Singaporeans a link to their past and heritage. The Urban Redevelopment Authority(URA) was formally made the Conservation Authority in 1989 and during the year, 10 areas, including Little India, Clarke Quay, Emerald Hill, Tanjong Pagar and Bukit Pasoh, came under the conservation plan. Even after a decade after its restoration, despite the building's spanking new facades, a sense of its historical character still lingers.

36. These terrace houses at Emerald Hill Road were built between 1901 and 1925. In 1981, the Urban Redevelopment Authority (URA) designated part of this area under the government conservation scheme. To preserve these unique early 20th century architecture, owners of these houses were urged to renovate their houses but to retain the original character and historic quality of these houses.

37. Straits Chinese residential terrace houses along Blair Road, constructed in the 1920s. What makes these terrace houses unique is that they were built with an eclectic style that blends Chinese, Malay, European and Colonial elements all into one.

38. What used to be warehouses and trading offices that lined the Singapore River bank are now restaurants, pubs and cafes after the Boat Quay area was renovated under the government's conservation plan.

39. Bumboats, which used to ply the river to transport rice, spices, rubber and other commodities, have now been given a new lease of life to become river taxis for tourists to cruise along the Singapore River.

40. Little India at Serangoon Road is the centre of the local Indian community. The streets are filled with many rich and vibrant elements of the Indian culture.

41. CHIJMES, at Victoria Street. This is a fine example of a unique blend of historical architecture and modern restoration. This four-acre site contains five neo-Gothic styled buildings which includes a Gothic chapel decorated with elegant stained glass panels and the former St. Nicholas Girl's School building and Caldwell House, which has a sunken forecourt, waterfalls and fountains. After restoration, this place retains its old charm and tradition even though pubs, restaurants and shops have replaced the former uses of these buildings.

42. Victoria Theatre was built in 1862 as the Singapore Town House and the Concert Hall on the left only opened in 1905. There was originally a gap between the two buildings and a clock tower was added to fill the gap much later.

44. The Fullerton Hotel is the result of a $400-million restoration work. This grand building was completed in 1928 and was formerly known as Fullerton Building. It was used to house The Exchange, The Chamber of Commerce, the Singapore Club and later the Comptroller of Income Tax and the General Post Office.

45. The Raffles Hotel was completed in 1887. It is the oldest and most famous hotel in Singapore. It was declared a national monument by the Singapore government in 1987. Raffles Hotel is well-recognised worldwide and it is considered one of the finest hotels in the world.

Living In Singapore

Few countries in the world can claim to be as successful as Singapore in providing public housing for its people. The Housing and Development Board, which was established in 1960, provides housing for more than 92 per cent of the population. The HDB lifestyle is distinctly Singaporean and there is no better way to experience a slice of life in Singapore than to make a trip to the HDB heartlands.

46. A new 30-storey flat in Toa Payoh Town. The Housing and Development Board of Singapore will build new 40 storey flats in the future in parts of Singapore which came under the new high-density plan.

47. Modern living along the river at Pasir Ris housing estate.

48. The Light Rapid Transit (LRT) System.

49A. Every housing estate is well planned and beautifully landscaped with flora and fauna.

49B. Toa Payoh Town Centre. Like many town centres, it offers many amenities for the residents' convenience. Most larger town centres have a shopping centre, food centre, supermarket, a library and even cineplexes.

49C. A newly completed flat in a new estate with a childrens' playground right below the block.

50B. There is at least one community club in each estate to serve the community. The club conducts regular classes and courses for residents and provides various forms of leisure activities for the residents to enhance greater interaction among residents.

50C. A group of old folks having a chat after doing a morning of marketing at a market in Toa Payoh estate.

50A. Sun Plaza, next to Sembawang train station. Many new estates have mega malls and shopping centres located close to the MRT stations.

51. New four and five-rooms flats ready to be occupied. Public housing in Singapore is affordable and preferred by many young couples as they cost only half or one third of the price of private housing.

52 and 53. New HDB flats in the new estates. To meet the increased demand for higher quality living, the Housing and Development Board introduced the Design Plus Scheme which engages private architects and contractors to build well-designed flats comparable in standard to private condominiums.

Singapore, The Garden City

There are more than half a million trees lining the roads of Singapore. Almost everywhere you go, you can find a shady tree to shield you from the heat of the tropical sun. This is the success of the Garden City campaign which started in the mid 1960s under the skilful management of The National Parks Board of the Ministry of National Development. Today the Singapore government spends about S$80 million a year to plant new trees and shrubs and to upkeep the Singapore's image as a clean and green city.

54 and 55. One of the largest parks in Singapore, Bishan Park is a beautiful park with lush greenery, lakes and bridges. Nature-loving residents appreciate having a vast garden right at their door steps; literally living in a garden city.

56A. Beautiful walkways along Bras Basah Road

56B. Bras Basah Park, is a 3.3 hectares city park at Bras Basah Road. The lawn and trees with wide extending branches provide cool shades making it an ideal setting for picnicking and relaxation.

57. Trees, shrubs and palm trees line the walkway along Stamford Road.

58.and 59. MacRitchie Reservoir at Thomson Road is a favourite spot for the health enthusiast.

Singapore Orchids

The National Flower of Singapore is Vanda Miss Joaquim. This exquisite orchid hybrid was discovered by Miss Agnes Joaquim in her garden in 1893, hence the name. The splendour and variety of the orchids that you see in Singapore today are products of the Singapore Botanic Garden' breeding programme which started in 1928.

Today, there are over 700 species and more than 2,100 quality hybrids which are 'masterpieces of art' created by the Garden's horticultural staff. The National Orchid Garden of Singapore now offers the largest display of orchids in the world.

Transportation In Singapore

Singapore strives to be an international business hub. And one way to achieve this is to have a world-class transport system that connects Singapore via air and sea links to the world. Today, Singapore is the world's busiest port in terms of shipping tonnage with shipping links to more than 700 ports worldwide. Singapore's Changi Airport is the airport with the most airlinks in the Asia Pacific region serving flights to and from 150 cities and 50 countries worldwide.

66. The Air Control Tower at Singapore Changi Airport.

67. The interior of the Departure Hall at Changi Airport Terminal Two.

coffee club

68. The Mass Rapid Transit (MRT) system is an electrically driven railway system.
    The 83-kilometre system has 49 stations.

69. Light Rapid Transit (LRT) trains in Bukit Panjang estate. The LRT system began operating in 1999 and trains shuttle between Choa Chu Kang MRT station and around the estate to provide residents with easy access to the MRT system.

70. The new Singapore Expo MRT Station was opened on 10 January 2001. Trains will shuttle between Tanah Merah Station and the Singapore Expo Station every 15 minutes. The station has a futuristic look with two spaceship-like roofs suspended above the platform.

71A. An underground platform at Toa Payoh MRT station.

71B. The interior of the new Singapore Expo Station.

71C. The interior of a MRT train.

71D. Stunning red steel structure above the platform at Jurong MRT Station.

Religions and Festivals

Singapore is a multi-cultural society. The different ethnic groups and their customs and festivals give Singapore a vibrant and rich cultural heritage. The Chinese forms 76 per cent of Singapore's 4-million population while the Malays and Indians constitute 13.9 per cent and 7.9 per cent of the total population respectively. The main religions are Buddhism, Taoism, Hinduism and Islam but more than half of the residents are Buddhists and Taoists. About 14.6 per cent of the population are Christians, and Muslims and Hindus comprised of 14.9 and 4 per cent of the population respectively.

72. Young boys participating in the temple's noviciate programme during the school holidays at Phor Kark See Temple.

73. The Dharma Hall at Phor Kark See Temple is also a Buddhist library. It has a wide collection of Buddhist scriptures and literature.

74. The Hall of Great Compassion at Phor Kark See Temple. It houses a large sculpture of the Avalokitesvara Bodhisattva or Kuan Yin who is well known for his limitless skilful means and great compassion.

75A. The Stupa of Ten Thousand Buddhas. It is uniquely designed, blending South-east Asian and modern architectural style. As you look up into the bell-shaped ceiling, you will see thousands of small Buddha statues lined round the roof all the way up to the tip of the tower's ceiling. These statues symbolise the immeasurable virtues of the Buddha.

75B. The Hall of Amrta Vinaya (Ambrosia Precepts). This is the place where monks receive their precepts. As precepts are like ambrosia that satisfies one's hunger and thirst, the Precepts Hall is hence called Amrta Vinaya, meaning ambrosia precepts in Pali.

75C. The bronze Buddha statue in the Hall of Ten Thousand Buddhas.

76.Thian Hock Keng Temple at Telok Ayer Street. The temple was first built in 1842 and was the focal point of prayers and gatherings of the Hokkien immigrants who came from Fujian province in south China. It was restored to its formal glory in 2001 after a S$3.5 million restoration project which involved the skills of 70 craftsmen from Fujian using the traditional post-and-beam method.

77. Another view of Thian Hock Keng Temple. Notice the elaborate gold patterns on the ceilings of the temple's corridor painstakingly carved by hand.

78. Cheng Huang Miao, a smaller temple next to Siong Lim Temple. Cheng Huang is the Minister of Hell who assist the King Yama (Hell Emperor) in punishing evil doers. On the 12th lunar month every year, devotees give thanks and offerings to the Minister of Hell. The 'bags' hanging on the walls shown in this picture are actually trays of neatly folded paper robes, offerings from devotees.

79. Siong Lim Temple was built in the late 19th century. The picture shows the Hall of Great Strength which is the main shrine hall of the temple. The words "great strength" refers to the Lord Buddha for his wisdom to eradicate the roots of suffering which are greed, hatred and delusion.

80A. Maitreya which means "loving kindness" is also known as the Buddha of the Future.

80B. Wei Tuo, the guardian of the temple and protector of the good doers. He holds a pestle, pointing vertically downwards and this implies that this temple is opened to the public. If the pestle is placed horizontally on his arms, this means that the temple is only opened to devotees of the same sect.

81. Sultan Mosque at North Bridge Road. The mosque, constructed in 1928, is intricately designed with a massive golden dome and a large prayer hall.

82. Al-Abbar Mosque at Telok Ayer Street. It is also known as Kuchu Palli which means "mosque hut" in Tamil.

83. St Andrew's Cathedral, situated at St Andrew's Road, was designed by Lieutenant-Colonel Ronald MacPherson in 1856.

84. Sri Mariamman Temple at South Bridge Road. Built in 1827, this is the oldest Hindu temple in Singapore. The temple is a popular venue for Hindu weddings and the annual fire-walking ceremony.

85. An Indian priest conducting poojas (making of offerings) to a Hindu goddess.

86. The Central Sikh Temple at Serangoon Road.

87A. Religious murals depicting a Sikh guru.

87B. A newly-wed Sikh couple waiting to be blessed in the temple.

88. A statue of the God of Wealth welcoming a new year.

89A. A busy street in Chinatown.

89B. Colourful and glittering posters with auspicious words written on them. The Chinese loves to buy these to hang or paste on the walls at home to usher in good luck during the Chinese Lunar New Year.

89C. A variety of golden and red-coloured new year decorations on sale in Chinatown.

90. What better way to get into the spirit of Chinese New Year than to immerse oneself into the festive crowd in Chinatown. The streets around the area are usually closed and stalls would line the streets, selling all sorts of traditional New Year goodies, clothing, shoes and household items.

91A, 91B, 91C:

The Festival of the Hungry Ghosts originates from the Taoist belief that the gates of hell are thrown open throughout the seventh month of the lunar year. During this period spirits are allowed to wander free. To appease these spirits, offerings of food, paper money, incense, paper cars and paper houses are made to the dead. To entertain these spirits, Chinese street operas and outdoor concerts are staged all over the island together with prayer sessions and banquets.

92A and 92B: The mid-Autumn Festival or the Mooncake Festival falls on the fifteen day of the eight lunar month. Eating mooncakes and displaying lanterns are marks of this festive tradition. Cashing in on the season are shrewd businessmen who hawk their wares as early as one month before the actual day.

92C. Another popular Chinese festival is the annual pilgrimage to Kusu Island. During this period Taoists travel to the Tua Pekkong Temple on the island to pray for prosperity, good luck and fertility. According to a legend, a turtle once saved two sailors – a Malay and a Chinese - from a ship-wrecked before it turned into an island.

93A. Thaipusam is celebrated by the Hindus in the month of January in honour of Lord Subramaniam. The highlight of the festival is the procession by devotees carrying Kavadis with their bodies pierced with spikes and skewers driven through their tongues and cheeks. Such a show of religious devotion requires spiritual preparation by fasting and praying.

93-B. A religious procession of a Hindu Goddess.

94

94A, 94B and 95:
Christmas is widely celebrated in Singapore even for the non-Christians. Parties are held everywhere and gifts are exchanged. During this season, the entire stretch of Orchard Road is transformed into a fairly land of lights.